BEST
DOLLAR
SAVING
DINNERS

BEST DOLLAR SAVING DINNERS

CHEAP AND EASY MEALS THAT TASTE GREAT

MONICA SWEENEY

For information about permission to reproduce selections from this book, write to Permissions, The Countryman Press, 500 Fifth Avenue, New York, NY 10110

For information about special discounts for bulk purchases, please contact W. W. Norton Special Sales at specialsales@wwnorton.com or 800-233-4830.

Library of Congress Cataloging-in-Publication Data

Names: Sweeney, Monica, author.
Title: Best dollar saving dinners : cheap and easy meals that taste great /Monica Sweeney.
Description: Woodstock, VT : The Countryman Press, a division of W. W. Norton & Company, [2016] | Includes bibliographical references and index.
Identifiers: LCCN 2015045125 | ISBN 9781581573916 (pbk. : alk. paper)
Subjects: LCSH: Quick and easy cooking. | Low-budget cooking. | LCGFT: Cookbooks. Classification: LCC TX833.5 .S944 2016 | DDC 641.5/12—dc23
LC record available at http://lccn.loc.gov/2015045125

The Countryman Press
www.countrymanpress.com

A division of W. W. Norton & Company, Inc.,
500 Fifth Avenue, New York, NY 10110
www.wwnorton.com

10 9 8 7 6 5 4 3 2 1

TO JOANNE,
FOR YOUR IMPROV IN THE KITCHEN.

BEST DOLLAR SAVING DINNERS
CONTENTS

Chapter Three: From the Skillet / 63

Chapter Four: From the Slow Cooker / 77

Chapter Five: Soups / 93

Chapter Six: Sandwiches, Salads, and More / 103

Introduction

You don't have to spend a lot of money to do dinnertime right. In fact, as far as I'm concerned, you really shouldn't spend a lot of money. There are countless ways to save your hard-earned cash while still providing your family with a hearty, satisfying meal at the end of the day. This book provides you with fifty "Dollar Saving Dinners" to feed a family of four to six people for just a few dollars (or less!) per individual serving. Also included are some extremely low-priced meals I like to call "Best Bargains." For these particular recipes, I include the dollar amount you can expect to spend per serving (based on grocery store prices in my area). These prices will of course vary by store and region, but they will give you a sense of how little you need to pay for a hearty dinner. Imagine all the grocery money you'd save by preparing these bargain meals for even a few days each week!

That's just the beginning of how this recipe book can help free up more of your money every month: cost-cutting is a state of mind, and getting to that state of mind means reflecting on how you shop for and store food, and even how you treat your leftovers. Most of us have buying and cooking habits that are more expensive than we realize. Whether you're guilty of tossing out a stripped-clean rotisserie chicken without boiling the bones for chicken stock, or have a knack for watching leftovers go bad because you get sick of the same old thing, it's a common habit to waste what could be reused. This book will give you helpful suggestions for repurposing those boring leftovers in new and exciting ways! In addition, I've provided a whole slew of savings tips to give you a head start as a Dollar Saving Dinner expert!

Savings Strategies for Winning Meals

BUY SMART

Buy big, buy on sale, and buy in-season. These are the three tried-and-true shopping rules for Dollar Saving Dinner. Nine times out of ten, that giant family pack of chicken wings is cheaper than the smaller portions. It may seem like more than you need, but it's easy enough to portion those wings into space-friendly freezer bags that you can squeeze into the corners of your freezer and enjoy another day. The savings are worth a few minutes of your time.

Be flexible. Don't go to the grocery store with a rigid list of items tied to specific meals. Allow sale items to inspire your weekly menu. Be most flexible with your meat and protein, since those items are usually the most expensive. If you're prepared to make a pork roast, but pork chops are on super sale, be ready and willing to make the swap and save big.

Pay attention to what's in season. Buy your fresh squash in the fall, your broccoli and cauliflower in the winter, and your spinach in the spring—or buy frozen vegetables as a rule and you'll save year round.

CONSIDER PORTION SIZE

The next time you sit down to dinner, take note of the way the food looks on your plate. Most of us tend to cover about half of our plate with meat and split the other half between starch and veggies. It takes time and commitment, but if you change the way you portion your food, you can avoid overspending and overeating. Consider how much meat you're accustomed to eating, for example. According to the American Heart Association, a serving of meat should weigh about 3 ounces, which (from a visual standpoint) is about the size of a computer mouse. Keep this in mind when you serve your Dollar Saving Dinners and be careful not to dole out excessive amounts of meat, as it's usually the most expensive part of the meal. Fill up on vegetables and whole grains instead and you'll balance your diet while you save money.

BE A FOOD RESCUER

There's a five-second rule for eating something that fell on the floor, but why not apply that same rule to food items before throwing them away? Before you toss that browning apple, that mildly squishy green pepper, or that picked-clean rotisserie chicken, stop and consider for five seconds whether there is still some part of it that can be salvaged. Slice up the better part of the apple for your kid's lunch tomorrow and squeeze in a little lemon juice to keep it from browning. Chop up the best portion of that bell pepper and freeze it for your next stir-fry. Taking the time to make the most of your purchased food means less waste, less unnecessary trips to the grocery store, and more spending money!

COOK IT SLOW, MAKE IT LAST

The slow cooker—or crockpot as some refer to it—wins the Dollar Saving Dinner kitchen appliance award for its money-saving powers. Even if you use a slow cooker once a week, you'll find that its effect on your weekly grocery bill is significant. For starters, having a slow cooker allows you to buy cheaper, tougher cuts of meat, since any meat cooked on low for 8 hours will soften to become deliciously tender. Secondly, it allows you to make larger portions of food that can be used all week, or frozen and saved for another day. Thirdly, using a slow cooker requires less power than using your oven, so you'll even save on your utility bill. In summary, slow cooker dinners + you = savings.

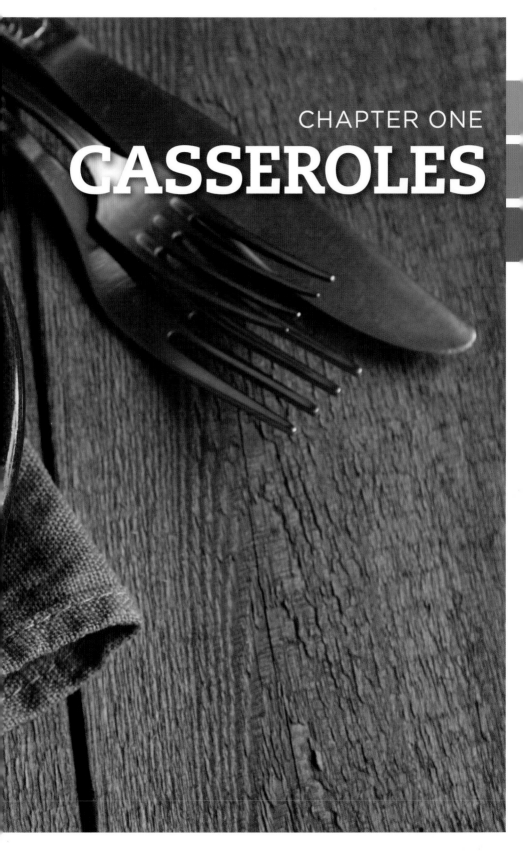

CHAPTER ONE
CASSEROLES

Cottage Pie

In the US, most of us know this as Shepherd's Pie, but the difference is in the meat. Cottage Pie is made with beef and Shepherd's Pie is made with lamb. For centuries, people have been filling up on this meat-and-potato casserole without feeling like they're skimping. That's because on a cold day, there's nothing better than biting into a warm cloud of creamy mashed potatoes, tender carrots, and seasoned ground beef.

Yield: 6 servings

3 tablespoons cooking oil, divided

1 pound ground beef

¾ cup onion, chopped

2 garlic cloves, minced

1 tablespoon tomato paste

½ cup beef broth

1½ teaspoons salt, divided

¼ teaspoon pepper

1 cup canned (or fresh cooked) carrots, sliced

8 medium potatoes, peeled and cubed

⅓ cup hot milk

1 cup (4 ounces) shredded cheddar cheese

2 egg whites

Preheat oven to 425°F. Grease a 7 x 11-inch baking dish. Add 2 tablespoons of oil to a large skillet. Add ground beef, onion, and garlic and cook until the meat is browned. Drain. In a separate bowl, whisk tomato paste and broth together. Add 1 teaspoon salt and all of pepper. Pour into pan with meat mixture and slowly mix. Cover bottom of greased baking dish with beef mixture. Scatter carrots over meat mixture. Cook potatoes in boiling salted water until tender; drain. Mash with milk, cheese, and remaining salt. Beat egg whites until stiff peaks form; fold into potatoes. Layer mashed potatoes over carrots in the baking dish. Bake uncovered for 15 minutes. Reduce heat to 350°F; bake 20 minutes longer.

Baked Manicotti with Ham and Spinach

Affordable meals don't have to be boring. While I can never replicate my Italian stepmom's classic manicotti recipe, this one turns the manicotti into tender, buttery casings with a savory spinach filling. This artful pasta casserole recipe has all the flavor of gourmet without the price.

Yield: 4 servings

SAUCE

2½ cups milk

4 tablespoons butter, divided

2 tablespoons flour

1 pinch nutmeg

½ teaspoon garlic powder

FILLING

1½ cups frozen spinach, boiled and drained

⅓ cup grated Parmesan cheese, divided

1 cup ham, chopped

½ teaspoon dried basil

Pinch of salt and pepper

2 eggs

1 box oven-ready Manicotti

Preheat oven to 375°F. Grease a 9 x 13-inch baking pan.

Continued . . .

To make the sauce: Bring milk to a boil in a small saucepan. Remove from heat. Melt 2 tablespoons of butter in a medium saucepan over medium heat. Add flour and stir for 2 minutes. Add heated milk to medium saucepan and whisk as you bring to a simmer. Season mixture with nutmeg and garlic powder. Pour 1 cup of sauce on bottom of greased baking pan.

To make the filling: Add spinach, half of the Parmesan cheese, and ham to food processor and process. Add basil, salt, and pepper. Beat eggs in medium bowl. Add spinach mixture to eggs. Mix well.

Bring a large pot of water to a boil. Cook manicotti for 3 minutes. Drain and arrange on a baking sheet. Spoon 2 tablespoons of filling into manicotti noodle and place in prepared baking dish. Repeat with all manicotti. Spread remaining cream sauce over manicotti. Sprinkle on remaining butter and Parmesan cheese. Bake for 30 minutes.

Fill up on sides that are rich in fiber (like spinach) and you can lessen the amount of expensive meat you would normally serve with a satisfying meal.

Turkey Lasagna

When in doubt, you can always depend on a pasta-heavy meal like lasagna to save you some serious dollars. If you make lasagna often enough that a variation is in order, try adding flavor and nutritional value with a layer of garlic-sautéed spinach (2 to 3 cups of thawed frozen spinach should do the trick). Use additional pasta sauce if you prefer your lasagna to be on the saucy side.

Yield: 9 servings

3 cups ricotta cheese

3 cups shredded mozzarella cheese

¾ cup grated Parmesan cheese

½ teaspoon oregano

2 eggs

1 pound ground turkey

1 (24-ounce) jar pasta sauce

1 box cooked lasagna noodles

Preheat the oven to 400°F. Stir the ricotta cheese, mozzarella cheese, ½ cup Parmesan cheese, oregano, and eggs in a medium bowl and set aside. In a medium-size saucepan over medium-high heat, brown the turkey. Drain. Pour the sauce into the saucepan with the turkey and stir. Spoon 1 cup browned meat into a 9 x 13-inch baking dish. Top with 4 lasagna noodles and about ¾ cups cheese mixture. Repeat twice. Top with the remaining 4 lasagna noodles, remaining meat mixture, and Parmesan cheese. Bake for 30 minutes or until top is bubbling.

Chicken and Broccoli Casserole

This is a simple, speedy recipe to prepare when you're rushing to make dinner and resisting the temptation to order take-out. With just five ingredients, it's easy to make this casserole and still stay within your weekly budget. For extra savings, divide this casserole into two smaller dishes so you can serve one and freeze the other for later.

Yield: 8 servings

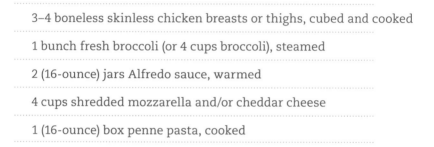

3–4 boneless skinless chicken breasts or thighs, cubed and cooked

1 bunch fresh broccoli (or 4 cups broccoli), steamed

2 (16-ounce) jars Alfredo sauce, warmed

4 cups shredded mozzarella and/or cheddar cheese

1 (16-ounce) box penne pasta, cooked

Preheat oven to 350°F. Add cooked chicken, broccoli, Alfredo sauce, and 2 cups cheese to saucepan and stir. Stir in cooked pasta. Spray or grease a 9 x 13-inch casserole dish. Empty saucepan mixture into baking dish. Sprinkle 2 cups cheese on top. Bake for about 10 minutes or until cheese melts.

Bacon & Ranch
Chicken Rollups

Changing the look of your dinners is one way to liven up your go-to recipes—and it doesn't cost a cent! This unique take on the traditional chicken casserole features miniature roll-ups loaded with shredded chicken, cooked bacon, and ranch dressing. It won't take long for this recipe to find its way into your weekly dinner line-up.

Yield: 6 servings

1 (8-ounce) package cream cheese, softened

2–3 tablespoons ranch dressing mix

2 cups shredded rotisserie or cooked chicken

1 cup Monterey Jack cheese, shredded

6 slices bacon, cooked and chopped

¼ cup scallions, chopped

1 egg, beaten with 1 teaspoon water

8 (8-inch) flour tortillas

1 tablespoon olive oil

Coarse salt

Preheat oven to 425°F and line a baking sheet with foil. In a large bowl, mix together the cream cheese and ranch seasoning. Add chicken, cheese, bacon, scallions, and egg mixture. Stir to combine. Spoon ⅓ cup of chicken mixture onto tortilla, leaving a ½-inch border around the edges. Fold in two sides and roll the tortilla with the filling inside. Repeat with remaining tortillas. Cut each one in half or into thirds and place seam-side down on baking sheet. Brush exposed tortilla with oil and sprinkle with salt. Bake for 15 to 18 minutes until golden brown. Serve ranch dressing on the side for dipping.

Cheesy Ham & Potato Casserole

This is a scrumptious choice for using up leftover ham or for any day of the week when you're craving a warm, layered entrée. Double up on the potatoes to thicken this casserole and stretch your dollars. For a creamier version, add 8 ounces of softened cream cheese to the pan when heating the cheese topping.

Yield: 4-6 servings

4 cups potatoes, sliced, peeled, and cooked

1½ cups ham, diced and cooked

1 cup mushrooms, sliced

⅓ cup butter, cubed

3 tablespoons all-purpose flour

1½ cups milk

1 cup shredded cheddar cheese

¾ teaspoon salt

Pinch of pepper

Fresh dill (for garnish)

Preheat oven to 350°F. Cover the bottom of a greased 9 x 13-inch baking dish with potatoes, ham, and mushrooms. In a saucepan, melt butter over medium heat; stir in flour until smooth. Gradually add milk. Bring to a boil; cook and stir for 2 minutes or until mixture is thick and bubbly. Add cheese, salt, and pepper; stir until the cheese is melted. Pour over potato mixture in baking dish. Bake, uncovered, for 25 to 30 minutes or until bubbling. Garnish with dill.

Check your local grocery store's sales online (or in the circular) before you make your meal plan for the week. Apps like Grocery Pal and Shop Savvy can also help you find the best deals.

Baked Ziti Pesto with Sundried Tomatoes

When your Dollar Saving Dinner is based around pasta, you can afford to throw in a few luxuries. This recipe features a lavish homemade pesto sauce and a healthy dose of sundried tomatoes. Whether you have a vegetarian or a pasta lover in your family, this dish aims to please.

Yield: 6 servings

1 box ziti or penne pasta (about 3 cups)

1 medium onion, chopped

3 large garlic cloves, minced

1 cup sundried tomatoes

¼ cup purchased pesto sauce

Salt and pepper, to taste

6 ounces mozzarella cheese, cubed

1 cup grated Parmesan cheese (about 3 ounces)

Preheat oven to 375°F. Spray 9 x 13-inch glass baking dish with nonstick spray. Boil pasta for amount of time specified on packaging. Sauté onion and garlic in saucepan over medium-high heat for about 5 minutes. Add sundried tomatoes and pesto. Season with salt and pepper if desired. Empty cooked, drained pasta into saucepan with pesto. Add mozzarella and ⅓ cup Parmesan. Transfer mixture to prepared baking dish. Sprinkle with remaining ⅔ cup Parmesan cheese. Bake until sauce bubbles and cheeses melt, about 30 minutes.

Tuna & Shells Casserole

This tuna casserole helps you avoid an extra trip to the grocery store by encouraging you to use the canned goods you already have in your pantry. To give this casserole extra crunch, try substituting shredded hash browns for breadcrumbs. This is a dinner that's affordable, easy, and slow cooker-friendly.

Yield: 4-5 servings

2 (6-ounce) cans tuna

2 (10-ounce) cans cream of mushroom soup

1 cup milk

1 cup fresh or frozen peas (thawed)

1 box shell pasta, cooked

¼ cup Parmesan cheese

2 cups breadcrumbs

BEST Bargain Alert $1.45 per serving!

Preheat oven to 350°F. Combine first six ingredients and 1½ cups of breadcrumbs in a large bowl; pour into an 7 x 11-inch greased baking dish. Sprinkle remaining breadcrumbs on top. Bake for 1 hour or until warmed through. To make this casserole in a slow cooker, combine all ingredients except pasta and add to slow cooker. Cook on low for 4 hours, adding pasta 20 minutes before serving.

Track your food spending. Use online software or a plain-old pen and paper to record how much you normally spend every week on food. That way, you know when a savings plan is working and when it's not.

Jumbo Stuffed Pasta Shells

In this meal, tender, jumbo-size pasta shells are packed full of sausage and immersed in a chunky red sauce. Depending on which is cheaper at the market, you can fill your shells with turkey, pork, or chicken sausage. Either way, this dish is sure to earn you rave reviews.

Yield: 4 servings

1 box jumbo pasta shells

1 pound fresh sausage links, casing removed

1 tablespoon garlic, minced

1 (14-ounce) can diced tomatoes

½ cup ricotta cheese

½ cup shredded mozzarella cheese

Pinch of salt and freshly ground pepper

½ teaspoon fresh parsley, chopped

Preheat oven to 350°F and fill a large bowl with cold water and ice, set aside. Bring a large pot of salted water to a boil. Add pasta shells and cook according to package directions. Drain well, then add to ice water until ready to stuff. Heat a large skillet over medium-high heat. Add sausage to skillet, then use a wooden spoon to break up the sausage; cook 5 to 6 minutes until browned. Add garlic and cook 30 seconds, then add tomatoes; cook 1 minute. Remove pan from heat and stir in ricotta cheese. Fill pasta shells with spoonfuls of pork filling and arrange in a greased baking dish (9 x 9-inch baking dish works well). Sprinkle tops with shredded cheese, salt and pepper, and parsley; bake in the oven 25 to 30 minutes until cheese has melted and tips of shells begin to crisp and brown.

Deep Dish Meat-Lovers Pizza

This Deep Dish Pizza Casserole is loaded with toppings and mozzarella and can be customized to your family's tastes. Store-bought dough is easy enough to find, but you can lower your costs further by making your own. For extra savings, use the veggies that are already hanging around in your fridge as toppings.

Yield: 6 servings

¾ cup mushrooms, sliced or chopped

½ cup fresh or frozen (thawed) green bell pepper, sliced

1 (10-ounce) can refrigerated pizza crust dough

6 ounces shredded mozzarella

½ teaspoon oregano

½ teaspoon onion powder

1 (15-ounce) can pizza sauce

¼ cup canned black olives

12–15 slices pepperoni

Preheat oven to 425°F. In a large skillet, brown mushrooms and peppers in oil. Set aside. Coat a 9 x 13-inch baking dish with cooking spray. Roll out pizza dough and press into bottom and halfway up the sides of baking dish. Cover with half of the cheese. Add oregano and onion powder seasoning to pizza sauce and pour sauce evenly over dough. Add remaining cheese, browned vegetables, olives, and pepperoni. Bake uncovered for 12 minutes or until crust is browned and cheese is melted. Cool 5 minutes before serving.

Fiesta Black Bean Enchiladas

Bring some spicy flair to your dinner table without breaking the bank with this enchilada-style bean casserole. Adjust the spiciness to your liking: whether you choose a mild salsa and hold the jalapeño or you challenge your palate with an extra-hot salsa and a fiery kick of pepper, this meal is bursting with flavor.

Yield: 8 servings

1 tablespoon vegetable oil

½ cup onion, chopped

1 teaspoon ground cumin

½ teaspoon garlic, crushed

1 cup frozen whole kernel corn, thawed

1¾ cups (your favorite) salsa

1 (15-ounce) can black beans, rinsed and drained

2 cups shredded Monterey Jack cheese

8 tortillas

½ teaspoon parsley (for garnish)

BEST Bargain Alert
98¢ per serving!

Heat oven to 350°F. Grease a 7 x 11-inch baking dish with cooking spray. Heat vegetable oil in skillet over medium heat, then cook onion, cumin, and garlic until onion is translucent. Add corn, ¾ cup salsa, beans, and 1 cup of the cheese. Remove from heat. Wrap a stack of 8 tortillas in tinfoil and warm for 3 minutes in the oven to soften. Place ¼ cup bean mixture along center of each tortilla. Roll up tightly, and place seam sides down in baking dish. Pour remaining 1 cup salsa over enchiladas. Sprinkle with remaining 1 cup cheese. Bake 25 to 30 minutes or until cheese is melted and sauce is bubbly. Garnish with parsley.

Beans, nuts, seeds, and eggs are all nutritious and affordable sources of protein. Consider adding them to the dinner menu at least one day a week.

Veggie Quiche

Don't forget to use eggs in place of meat every now and then for a change of pace and a whole lot of savings. Vegetarians and egg lovers alike will appreciate the warm, fluffy, veggie-rich filling of this dinnertime quiche. Serve it on its own or with a side of your favorite crisp veggies.

Yield: 8–10 servings

1 tablespoon cooking oil

¼ cup onion, chopped

¼ cup green bell pepper, chopped

1 tablespoon all-purpose flour

¼ teaspoon salt

¼ teaspoon nutmeg

¼ teaspoon black pepper

¼ cup tomato, chopped

1 cup broccoli, finely chopped, steamed

1 (9-inch) frozen piecrust, thawed

½ cup shredded cheddar cheese

2 eggs, slightly beaten

¾ cup milk

¾ cup sour cream

Dill (for garnish)

Preheat oven to 400°F. Heat oil in large frying pan. Add onion and green pepper and cook until softened. Add flour and cook for 2 minutes, stirring frequently. Stir in salt, nutmeg, and pepper. Stir in tomato and broccoli. Empty vegetables over piecrust and top with cheddar cheese. Combine eggs, milk, and sour cream until smooth. Pour over cheese. Bake for 20 minutes, reduce temperature to 350°F, and bake 30 to 35 minutes or more until inserted knife comes out clean. Sprinkle with dill if desired.

Chicken Pot Pie

Buying chicken pot pie at the grocery store will usually cost you more than a few dollars a serving, and it never tastes as good as this homemade version. Make this warm, flaky comfort food even more affordable by using yesterday's roasted chicken. Because chicken pot pie reheats so well, there's no risk of wasting the leftovers!

Yield: 5 servings

3 medium carrots, sliced

2 medium red potatoes, cut into ½-inch cubes

¼ cup butter, cubed

¼ cup all-purpose flour

2 cups chicken broth

1 teaspoon dried thyme

¼ teaspoon nutmeg

½ teaspoon salt

½ teaspoon pepper

2 cups boneless, skinless chicken thigh meat, cooked

1 cup frozen peas, thawed

2 (9-inch) piecrusts

Place the carrots and potatoes in a large saucepan, and cover with water. Bring to a boil, then reduce heat, cover, and cook for 10 to 15 minutes or until vegetables are tender. Meanwhile, in a small saucepan, melt butter over medium heat, then stir in flour until smooth. Gradually add the broth, thyme, nutmeg, salt, and pepper. Bring to a boil; cook and stir for 2 minutes or until thickened. Drain vegetables and place in a large bowl; stir in the white sauce, chicken, and peas. Preheat oven to 375°F. Add pie-filling mixture to one piecrust. Place second crust over filling; trim, seal, and flute edges. Cut slits in top. Bake for 25 to 30 minutes or until crust is golden brown and filling is bubbly.

Canned and frozen fruits and veggies are more economical than the fresh variety, and some have even more nutrients than their fresh counterpart.

CHAPTER TWO

FROM THE OVEN

Honey-Barbecue
Chicken Tenders

Dress up your usual chicken tenders with this flavorful alternative. From their crunchy, breaded exterior to their sweet and tangy centers, you'll savor every bite. Give this recipe even more savings power when you make it from value packs of chicken tenderloins purchased at your favorite bulk wholesale store. Add a side of cooked vegetables and golden brown french fries to this meal and enjoy.

Yield: 4 servings

¾ cup your favorite BBQ sauce, plus more for dipping

¼ cup honey

1 pound chicken tenderloins

½ cup flour

1 teaspoon salt

½ teaspoon black pepper

2 large eggs

1½ cups breadcrumbs

Combine barbecue sauce and honey in a large bowl. Cut chicken tenderloins in half lengthwise. Add the chicken strips to the bowl and coat with sauce. Cover tightly and marinate in the refrigerator for at least 30 minutes. Preheat oven to 400° F. Coat a baking sheet with cooking oil spray. Combine flour, salt, and pepper in a shallow dish. Beat eggs in another shallow dish. Pour breadcrumbs into a third shallow dish. Coat each chicken strip in flour, then egg, then breadcrumbs, and place chicken strips onto baking sheet. Spray cooking oil directly onto strips and bake. Flip tenders after 10 minutes, and cook for 10 more minutes or until white and flaky in the middle. Serve with BBQ sauce for dipping.

Rosemary Roasted Chicken & Potatoes

With one taste of the crispy, golden skin of this rosemary-lemon chicken, you'll be a lifetime fan of this recipe. Prepare this juicy roasted chicken early in the week, and use any leftover meat for a chicken salad for lunch throughout the week. Don't forget to save the bones for hearty, healthy bone broth!

Yield: 4–6 servings

3½ pounds bone-in, skin-on chicken parts

½ cup olive oil

¼ cup fresh rosemary

¼ cup fresh lemon juice

10 garlic cloves, sliced thin

Kosher salt and freshly ground black pepper, to taste

1 pound golden russet potatoes, quartered

1 lemon, sliced

BEST
Bargain Alert
$1.56
per serving!

Toss chicken with oil, rosemary, lemon juice, garlic, and salt and pepper in bowl. Marinate for 1 hour. Heat oven to 475°F. Spray a 9 x 13-inch baking dish with cooking spray. Arrange chicken pieces skin side up in baking dish; add potatoes and lemon slices to dish; drizzle with extra marinade from bowl. Roast 20 minutes. Flip. Roast 15 to 20 more minutes.

Give your leftovers a makeover so that you're more excited to eat them. Burritos, omelets, and soups are all terrific ways to repurpose yesterday's meal.

Cajun Chicken & Bacon with Rice

Saving money doesn't mean cooking boring dinners. This Cajun-style recipe is the perfect example of an affordable meal that's rich with flavor without being too heavy on the meat (or too demanding on the wallet). Adjust the cayenne pepper to suit your family's spice tolerance and relish in this quintessential showcase of Louisiana-style home cooking.

Yield: 4–6 servings

2 cups uncooked rice

1 cup frozen peas, thawed

2–3 boneless, skinless chicken breasts, cut into 1-inch pieces

2 teaspoons cooking oil

4 tablespoons butter

¾ cup onion, chopped

⅓ cup flour

½ teaspoon cayenne pepper

2 cups chicken broth

1 cup heavy cream

1 (2-ounce) jar diced pimientos

Pinch of thyme

1 tablespoon fresh chives, chopped

3 slices bacon, cooked (optional)

Preheat oven to 375°F. Prepare rice according to package directions, stir in peas and set aside. In medium skillet, brown chicken breast chunks in oil; set aside. Melt butter in large skillet over medium heat. Add onion and cook for several minutes; stir in flour and cayenne pepper. Add broth and cream; cook

5 minutes or until sauce thickens. Remove from heat and stir in pimientos and thyme. Mix together chicken, rice, and sauce in a large bowl, then dump into a greased 7 x 11-inch casserole dish. Bake for 30 to 35 minutes, or until chicken is cooked through. Top with chives and chunks of bacon (if desired).

Lemon Roasted Chicken Drumsticks

A delicious lemon-tarragon rub makes all the difference in this crowd-pleasing recipe that transforms everyday roasted chicken drumsticks into a new specialty to call your own. You can use just about any cut of chicken to bring this recipe to life, so purchase what's on sale and roast it over a bed of carrots and potatoes for a supremely successful Dollar Saving Dinner.

Yield: 5 servings

LEMON RUB

1 tablespoon lemon zest

2 tablespoons lemon juice

1 tablespoons tarragon

2 tablespoons unsalted butter, softened

½ teaspoon salt, plus additional to season

½ teaspoon black pepper, plus additional to season

ROAST

2½ pounds (skin-on) chicken thighs and drumsticks

6–8 small Yukon gold potatoes, cut in half

3 carrots, peeled and cut

Preheat the oven to 450°F.

Make lemon rub: Whisk together ingredients for lemon rub and set aside.

Roast chicken: Rinse the chicken and pat dry. Generously sprinkle with salt and pepper and place in roasting pan with potatoes and carrots. With a pas-

try brush, applylemon butter to skin of chicken and drizzle over potatoes and carrots. Cook for 35 minutes, or until internal temperature is at least 185°F. Remove from the oven and let sit 10 minutes before serving.

Make herbs last longer by placing them in a glass of water in the fridge. Position a plastic bag over the top and they'll stay even fresher.

Teriyaki Chicken Wings & Ginger Rice

This recipe makes good use of one of the most dollar-friendly cuts of chicken. The tangy teriyaki sauce turns these wings into an instant favorite. Serve them over a bed of ginger rice with a small salad and you've got a meal that's superb, simple, and thrifty. If you'd rather make them in your slow cooker, just add the broiled chicken and homemade teriyaki sauce to your crockpot and cook on high for 2 to 3 hours or on low for 5 to 6 hours.

Yield: 6 servings

CHICKEN

3 pounds chicken wings

1 large onion, chopped

1 cup brown sugar

1 cup soy sauce

¼ cup dry sherry or ¼ cup chicken broth

2 teaspoons fresh ginger, minced

1 tablespoon honey

1 garlic clove, minced

RICE

2 tablespoons unsalted butter

4 tablespoons fresh ginger, minced, peeled

2 cups rice, rinsed

3 cups chicken stock or broth

1 teaspoon salt

For the chicken: Rinse chicken and pat dry. Place wings on broiler pan. Broil on low 4 to 5 inches from heat for about 10 minutes per side or until chicken is lightly browned. Place broiler chicken in 7 x 11-inch baking dish. In medium-size bowl, mix together onion, brown sugar, soy sauce, cooking sherry (or chicken broth), ginger, honey, and garlic. Pour mixture over chicken wings. Bake at 350°F for about 30 minutes.

For the rice: In a medium saucepan, melt the butter. Add the ginger, rice, stock, and salt and bring to a boil. Cover and let simmer 12 minutes or until liquid is absorbed. Fluff and serve.

Italian Turkey Meatloaf

Fill your kitchen with the comforting scent of oven-baked meatloaf. Ground turkey makes this old fashioned meatloaf slightly more affordable, but you can also lessen the cost by substituting homemade breadcrumbs for the kind that come in a can. Take stale or dry bread (or bake it at 200°F for an hour to dry it out yourself) and process it in your food processor until you have the amount of crumbs you need. Serve with a salad or a side of green beans.

Yield: 5 servings

1 cup onion, finely chopped

½ cup grated Parmesan cheese

¾ cup Italian breadcrumbs

½ tablespoon garlic, minced

1 large egg, lightly beaten

1 tablespoon tomato paste

¾ teaspoon table salt

½ teaspoon freshly ground black pepper

2 (8-ounce) cans tomato sauce

1 pound ground turkey

Preheat oven to 375°F. Stir together the first 5 ingredients in a large bowl. In a separate bowl, combine tomato paste, salt, pepper, and 1 can tomato sauce; stir into first mixture. Add ground turkey to breadcrumb mixture and combine using hands. Line a 9 x 5-inch loaf pan with heavy-duty aluminum foil; coat lightly with cooking spray. Add meatloaf mixture to pan. Place pan on a foil-lined baking sheet. Bake for 15 minutes. Drizzle remaining can tomato sauce over meatloaf. Bake 30 more minutes or until meatloaf reaches internal temperature of 165°F.

Replenish your spices and canned goods at dollar stores and discount stores. Their prices on these items are often lower than grocery store prices.

Roasted Chicken with Orange Cranberry Sauce

Let Thanksgiving come to your home again and again with this frugal but festive family meal. This recipe adds a twist of orange to your traditional roasted chicken and homemade cranberry sauce for a uniquely satisfying dinner. Serve with a side of stuffing or mashed potatoes.

Yield: 4-6 servings

CHICKEN

1 whole chicken (about 4 pounds)

½ teaspoon kosher salt

¼ teaspoon black pepper

1 orange, quartered

SAUCE

½ cup fresh squeezed orange juice

½ cup fresh or frozen cranberries, thawed

2 tablespoons sugar

½ cup chicken broth

1½ teaspoons cornstarch

2 tablespoons water

2 oranges, peeled, sectioned and seeded

For the chicken: Preheat oven to 450°F. Rinse chicken with cold water; pat dry. Remove giblets and neck if necessary. Loosen skin and rub salt and pepper underneath. Place orange quarters inside chicken cavity. Roast chicken, breast side down, on a roasting pan for 25 minutes. Reduce oven temperature to 350°F. Flip chicken so it's breast side up; bake for 1 hour or until thermometer reads 180°F.

For the sauce: Mix together the orange juice, cranberries, and sugar in a medium saucepan over medium heat. Cook 5 minutes or until cranberries pop; add chicken broth. Combine the cornstarch and water in a small dish, and add to the cranberry mixture. Bring to a boil and cook for 1 minute, stirring constantly. Remove from heat. Place sections of orange in food processor and process until evenly chopped. Stir processed oranges into cranberry sauce. Serve over chicken.

Glazed Ham with Sweet Potatoes & Carrots

Saving money is as simple as buying large cuts of meat you can bake, enjoy, and save as leftovers. This simple recipe for glazed ham becomes even more of a dollar saver when you use the leftovers in tomorrow's breakfast omelet or in a Cheesy Ham and Potato Casserole (page 26) later in the week.

Yield: 6 servings

1 (2–3 pound) cured ham

1 large sweet potato, cubed

¾ cup baby carrots

1 tablespoon apple cider vinegar

1 tablespoon balsamic vinegar

1 tablespoon honey

1 tablespoon molasses

¼ teaspoon allspice

¼ cup water

Preheat the oven to 375°F. Place the ham in a baking dish and spread the sweet potatoes and carrots around it. In a small bowl, whisk together the apple cider vinegar, balsamic vinegar, honey, molasses, allspice, and water. Pour over the ham and vegetables. Cover the baking dish with aluminum foil and bake for 45 minutes to 1 hour.

Store your leftovers in clear containers so that you're less likely to ignore or forget about them.

Balsamic Pork Tenderloin & Roasted Brussels Sprouts

A basic pork tenderloin gets a worthy makeover with the addition of a balsamic reduction glaze. Pair this less expensive cut of meat with a flavorful vegetable, such as roasted Brussels sprouts, and you've got a winning formula. This recipe is also delicious when made in a slow cooker: just add a cup of chicken broth to the balsamic vinegar and allow the tenderloin to cook in the juices on low for 6 to 8 hours.

Yield: 4 servings

1¼ cups balsamic vinegar

2 tablespoons sugar

1 pound pork tenderloin

4 cups Brussels sprouts

1 teaspoon kosher salt

1 teaspoon coarse ground black pepper

2 teaspoons basil

½ teaspoon thyme

1 teaspoon olive oil

Preheat oven to 475°F. Bring balsamic vinegar to a boil in a small saucepan over medium-high heat. Reduce heat to medium once boiling and continue to cook, stirring often, until liquid is reduced by about half. Remove from heat and stir in sugar until dissolved. Set aside. Place tenderloin on greased cooking sheet, with Brussels sprouts surrounding it. Sprinkle tenderloin and Brussels sprouts with salt, pepper, basil, and thyme. Drizzle olive oil on Brussels sprouts. Bake for ten minutes, flip tenderloin, and bake 10 to 15 minutes more, or until no longer pink in the center. Allow to rest 5 to 10 minutes before slicing. Drizzle with balsamic reduction and serve.

CHAPTER THREE

FROM THE SKILLET

Southern Rice Pilaf with Ground Pork

In terms of versatility, this dish is a star player in your weekly lineup. The saffron in Spanish (yellow) rice offers up the most flavor, but you can also use brown or white rice if preferred. Vary the meat according to what's on sale at the grocery store: ground beef, pork, or turkey all work well in this recipe. Don't forget to wrap the leftovers (if there are any) in a tortilla for a grab-and-go lunch.

Yield: 4 servings

1 pound ground pork, beef, or turkey

¼ cup butter

1 cup onion, chopped

½ cup mushrooms, sliced

2 cups yellow rice, uncooked

1 teaspoon garlic, minced

1 tablespoon fresh parsley, chopped

½ teaspoon Creole seasoning (or a pinch of cayenne pepper)

Pinch of kosher salt

¼ teaspoon black pepper

3 cups chicken stock, chicken broth, or water

Cook the ground meat in a medium skillet, drain, remove from skillet, and set aside. Melt the butter in the same skillet, add the onion and mushrooms and sauté for about 5 minutes. Add the rice and cook until lightly browned. Add the drained meat and the remaining ingredients to the skillet; bring to a boil, reduce heat to simmer, cover, and let cook about 15 minutes or until most of the liquid has been absorbed into the rice. Fluff rice, empty into a serving bowl, and serve warm.

American Beef Goulash

This Americanized ground beef "stew" is an old family favorite. This recipe is picky-eater-friendly because of its simple ingredients, but it can also be dressed up with the addition of ripe tomatoes and zesty spices.

Yield: 4 servings

BEST
Bargain Alert
$1.42
per serving!

¾–1 pound ground beef

1 large onion, chopped fine

1 garlic clove, chopped

1 cup grape tomatoes, halved, or canned diced tomatoes

1 (15-ounce) can tomato sauce

1 tablespoon Worcestershire sauce

1 teaspoon salt (or more, to taste)

Pepper, to taste

2 cups elbow macaroni

Brown the ground beef in a large pan over medium heat. Add onion, and cook 5 minutes or until onion is translucent. Add garlic, tomatoes, tomato sauce, Worcestershire sauce, salt, and pepper to the beef mixture. Reduce heat and simmer 20 minutes. While the beef mixture cooks, boil the pasta until al dente. Add the macaroni to the beef mixture, stir well, and simmer another 15 minutes, covered. If too watery, remove lid and cook until sauce thickens.

Chicken Fajita Stir-Fry

End your day on a high note with this spicy fajita stir-fry. This southwestern specialty is a thrifty alternative to plain old chicken and vegetables. Serve over rice or wrapped in warm tortillas.

Yield: 4 servings

1 tablespoon chili powder

1 teaspoon cumin

1 teaspoon paprika

¼ teaspoon cayenne pepper

¼ teaspoon garlic powder

1 teaspoon salt

1 teaspoon ground black pepper

3 tablespoons olive oil, divided

1 pound boneless, skinless chicken breast, sliced into strips

2 bell peppers, sliced

1 onion, thinly sliced

8 small tortillas

Preheat oven to 250°F to warm tortillas. In a small bowl, whisk together chili powder, cumin, paprika, cayenne pepper, garlic powder, salt, and pepper. Set aside. Heat 1 tablespoon olive oil in a skillet or wok over medium-high heat. Add chicken strips and season with ¾ of fajita seasoning. Cook seasoned chicken, peppers, and onion in remaining oil for about 7 minutes, or until chicken is browned. Stir in remaining fajita seasoning. Wrap tortillas in tin foil and place in oven. To assemble fajitas, fill tortillas with chicken, peppers, and onions.

You get more for your money when you store your veggies with care. Wrap greens in a paper towel and place them in a plastic bag in your refrigerator to keep them fresher longer.

Herb-Crusted Skillet Pork Chops

With the right seasoning, a basic pork chop can be transformed into a savory main course. This recipe gets it right every time, thanks to a lemon-basil marinade that amplifies the flavor. Round out the meal with a side of applesauce and steamed, buttered baby carrots.

Yield: 4 servings

½ cup freshly squeezed lemon juice

⅓ cup cooking oil, plus more for sautéing

1 teaspoon rosemary

⅓ cup crushed basil

4 garlic cloves, sliced thin

1 teaspoons kosher salt

Freshly ground black pepper

6 boneless pork chops

In a shallow dish or pan, combine lemon juice, cooking oil, rosemary, basil, garlic, salt, and pepper. Lay pork chops in the marinade mixture in a single layer, flip to coat, and set aside for about 15 minutes at room temperature or up to 2 hours in the refrigerator. Preheat a large skillet over medium-high heat and add oil. Pat the chops dry, season with salt and pepper, and cook in skillet until crisp and brown, about 4 minutes on each side or until internal temperature is 160°F.

Know your cuts of meat and you'll get the best value. For example, choose pork rib chops over pork loin chops because they offer more meat per pound.

Garlic Chicken & Broccoli Rotini

This Dollar Saving Dinner is perfect for a busy weekday. Let the warm, garlic-infused chicken and pasta simmer on low and fill your kitchen with its enticing aroma. Buy your chicken breasts in a family value pack to maximize savings, or use boneless, skinless chicken thighs to stretch your dollar even further.

Yield: 6 servings

2 teaspoons vegetable oil

4 skinless, boneless chicken breasts or thighs cut into 1-inch cubes

2 cups fresh or frozen broccoli, chopped

1 (14.5-ounce) can chicken broth

1 (10.5-ounce) can condensed cream of chicken soup

1 teaspoon pepper

2 garlic cloves, minced (or ½ teaspoon garlic powder)

2 cups rotini pasta, uncooked

1 cup shredded cheddar cheese

Heat oil in skillet over medium-high heat. Add chicken and cook until no longer pink, about 2 to 3 minutes. Add broccoli, broth, soup, pepper, garlic, and pasta. Bring to a boil. Reduce heat to lowest setting, cover, and simmer for 15 to 20 minutes, stirring occasionally, until pasta is tender. If pasta looks dry, add a small amount of water. Melt shredded cheese over the top before serving.

Pork Strips & Veggie Stir-Fry

Stir-fry dishes are always a safe bet for savings, since they encourage you to make healthy vegetables the focus of your meal instead of the meat, which is generally the most expensive component. This scrumptious stir-fry features strips of honey-marinated pork plus oodles of tender onions, bell peppers, mushrooms, and broccoli, for a colorful and nutritious array of flavors and textures. Serve over rice if desired.

Yield: 4 servings

⅔ cup chicken broth

2 tablespoons cornstarch, divided

3 tablespoons soy sauce, divided

½ teaspoon chili powder, optional

2 tablespoons honey

1 (1-pound) pork tenderloin or chops, trimmed and cut into strips

1 tablespoon canola oil, divided

2 cups mushrooms, sliced

1 cup onion, chopped

1 cup broccoli, chopped

1 tablespoon fresh ginger, peeled and grated

2 garlic cloves, minced

1 cup yellow or red bell pepper, chopped

Combine chicken broth, 1 tablespoon cornstarch, 2 tablespoons soy sauce, chili powder (optional), and honey in a small bowl, and set aside. Combine pork, remaining 1 tablespoon cornstarch, and the remaining 1 tablespoon soy sauce in a bowl, tossing well to coat. Heat 2 teaspoons oil in a large nonstick skillet over medium-high heat. Add pork and sauté until browned. Remove pork and set aside. Add remaining 1 teaspoon oil to pan. Sauté mushrooms, onion, and

broccoli. Stir in ginger, garlic, and bell pepper. Stir in pork. Add reserved broth mixture to pan. Bring to a boil; cook 1 minute or until thick, stirring constantly.

Use the latest apps to keep leftovers from going to waste. The app BigOven, for example, lets you enter your leftover ingredients and then finds side dish, dinner, and dessert recipes that put them to use!

CHAPTER FOUR

FROM THE SLOW COOKER

Slow Cooker Chicken & Dumplings

Nothing stretches the dollar and soothes the soul like a bowlful of chicken and dumplings. This recipe goes straight from the slow cooker to your table. Expect it to disappear almost immediately!

Yield: 6 servings

CHICKEN

2 garlic cloves, minced

1 medium yellow onion, diced

1 whole bay leaf

1 teaspoon dried basil

1 teaspoon dried thyme

Freshly cracked pepper

4 cups water

1 large (¾ pound) chicken breast

1 teaspoon salt (plus more to taste)

DUMPLINGS

1½ cups all-purpose flour

1½ teaspoons baking powder

½ teaspoon salt

½ tablespoon dried parsley

¾ teaspoon sugar

6 tablespoons cold butter, cubed

½ cup milk

For the chicken: Add the garlic, onion, bay leaf, basil, thyme, pepper, and water to slow cooker and stir to combine. Add chicken and cook on high for 4 hours or low for 8 hours. Remove the cooked chicken from the broth and shred with two forks. Return the chicken to the slow cooker and stir in salt. Set slow cooker to high and cover.

For the dumplings: In a medium bowl, combine the flour, baking powder, salt, parsley, and sugar. Mix well. Add butter and incorporate into the dry ingredients using a pastry cutter. Add the milk and stir until mixture forms a paste. Drop heaping spoons of batter into the slow cooker with the cooked chicken. Return the lid to the slow cooker and let dumplings cook 20 minutes before serving.

Slow Cooker
Pot Roast

A crafty cook knows how to take a few shortcuts in the interest of time and money without sacrificing on flavor. This simple slow cooker pot roast recipe will satisfy a large family and then some! Freeze the leftovers so you can enjoy it again any time you want.

Yield: 10 servings

½ cup steak sauce

½ cup water

1 (9-ounce) package onion-mushroom soup mix

1 (approximately 2½-pound) boneless beef chuck eye roast

1 pound potatoes

1 (16-ounce) bag baby carrots

1 (16-ounce) bag green beans

1 onion, thickly sliced

Mix first 3 ingredients until blended. Place meat in slow cooker; top with vegetables and sauce. Cover with lid. Cook on low for 8 to 9 hours (or on high for 6 to 7 hours).

Find affordable substitutes for expensive recipe ingredients. For example, cranberry juice and chicken stock can both be used in place of red wine.

Slow Cooker Chicken Stroganoff

Just because you're on a budget doesn't mean that you can't enjoy a sensational dish like beef stroganoff. This recipe replaces the pricey beef with moist chicken thigh meat simmered in a golden-brown mushroom-and-onion gravy. The result is a palate-pleasing variation on a classic!

Yield: 4 servings

¼ cup chicken stock

1 (10.5-ounce) can cream of mushroom soup

2 cups mushrooms, sliced

1 cup onions, chopped

4 boneless, skinless chicken thighs

1 cup sour cream

¼ cup flour

Salt and pepper, to taste

1 (12-ounce) bag egg noodles, cooked

Place chicken stock, mushroom soup, mushrooms, and onions in the slow cooker and stir. Add chicken thighs. Cover and cook on high for 3 to 4 hours (or 7 to 9 hours on low). In a separate bowl, mix the sour cream and flour. Half an hour before serving stroganoff, add sour cream mixture and stir until chicken breaks into smaller pieces. Add salt and pepper to taste. Continue to cook for 30 minutes on low. Serve chicken and sauce over cooked noodles.

Slow Cooker Barbecue Brisket

When you're looking for affordable cuts of meat, look no further than the beef brisket. Avoided by less savvy buyers, this tough cut of meat can be delightfully tender when braised in liquid over low heat. Thanks to the braising power of your slow cooker, you can turn a value-priced brisket into a delicious Dollar Saving Dinner. Serve it warm with potato salad and cornbread on the side.

Yield: 6 servings

3 tablespoons packed light brown sugar

1½ tablespoons chipotle chili powder

1½ teaspoons ground cumin

½ teaspoon celery salt

1 garlic clove, minced

Kosher salt and freshly ground pepper

1 (3–4 pound) beef brisket, trimmed of fat

2 tablespoons Worcestershire sauce

1½ cups barbecue sauce

In a small bowl, combine the brown sugar, chili powder, cumin, celery salt, garlic, and salt and pepper. Apply rub to exterior of brisket, then place brisket in slow cooker (you may have to cut it into 2 pieces to do so). Combine Worcestershire sauce and barbecue sauce in a small bowl. Pour over the brisket. Cover and cook on low, 10 to 12 hours. Remove the brisket and let cool. Slice across the grain and serve.

Organize and label frozen leftovers with care. The easier it is to identify what's there (and remove it without an avalanche), the more likely you are to use it.

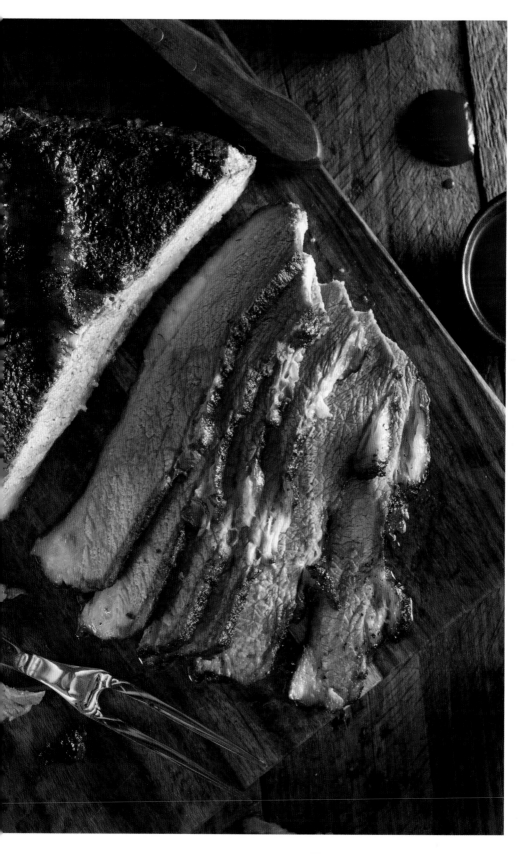

Slow Cooker Bacon Mac 'N Cheese

There's no better indulgence than a bowlful of creamy mac 'n cheese. This bacon-blended variety of mozzarella and cheddar mac 'n cheese, with a sprinkling of chives, is delicious to the last spoonful. I like to use turkey bacon because it's often a lot cheaper than pork bacon, but either option works well. Have some fun varying the cheese in this recipe: Smoky cheddar and pepper jack can give this dish a little extra gusto.

Yield: 4 servings

1 box elbow or fusilli pasta

2 cups shredded mozzarella cheese

2 cups shredded sharp cheddar cheese

3 slices cooked bacon, crumbled

2 eggs, lightly beaten

1 (12-ounce) can evaporated milk

1½ cups whole milk

1 teaspoon salt

½ teaspoon pepper

1 tablespoon chives (optional)

Spray interior of slow cooker with non-stick cooking spray. Place pasta, shredded cheeses, bacon, eggs, evaporated milk, milk, salt, and pepper in slow cooker; stir to combine. Cover and cook on high for 1½ hours, stirring occasionally. Reduce heat to low and cook 30 minutes or until pasta is tender and liquid is absorbed. Sprinkle with chives if desired and serve.

Slow Cooker Pork Cacciatore

This unique variation on the traditional Chicken Cacciatore takes a budget-friendly cut of pork and pairs it with a "hunter-style" onion, herb, and tomato sauce. What's ideal about this recipe is that you can use almost any kind of meat for the main course. Allow this week's grocery store bargains to guide your decision and you'll save even more!

Yield: 4 servings

4 boneless pork chops

2 tablespoons vegetable oil

1 onion, chopped

1 (28-ounce) jar pasta sauce

2 tomatoes, chopped

½ cup red wine vinegar

2 garlic cloves, minced

1 teaspoon Italian seasoning

½ teaspoon dried basil

2 cups rice, cooked

In a large skillet, brown chops over medium-high heat. Place in slow cooker. Add oil to skillet and cook onion over medium heat until translucent. Stir in pasta sauce, tomatoes, and vinegar. Season with garlic, Italian seasoning, and basil. Pour sauce over pork chops in slow cooker. Cook on low for 7 to 8 hours. Serve with a side of rice.

Make a double batch of this recipe and you'll save time and energy, as well as money.

Slow Cooker Fettuccine Alfredo

Treat your family to a plateful of chicken and noodles with creamy garlic Alfredo sauce. The pasta is filling, so there's no need to use an excess of chicken in this recipe. Consider using boneless, skinless chicken thighs for added savings.

Yield: 6 servings

2 (8-ounce) packages of cream cheese, softened

4 boneless, skinless chicken breasts or thighs

2 (10-ounce) cans cream of chicken soup

1¾ cups water

1 pouch Italian dressing mix

¾ teaspoon garlic powder

Dash of salt and pepper

2 (12-ounce) bags Fettuccine noodles

1 pinch Parmesan cheese (optional)

1 pinch fresh parsley

Spread the cream cheese on the bottom of the slow cooker. Place chicken breasts or thighs on top. In a separate bowl whisk together cream of chicken soup with water, dressing pouch, and garlic powder. Add salt and pepper. Pour sauce mixture over chicken. Cook on low for 4 hours. Remove chicken and cut into smaller pieces. Before returning chicken to slow cooker, whisk sauce in bottom of slow cooker to remove lumps.

Return chicken to slow cooker. Cook for 20 minutes. Cook noodles separately in a saucepan and serve together. Sprinkle with Parmesan cheese and fresh parsley if desired.

CHAPTER FIVE

SOUPS

Texas Ground Turkey Chili

This robust slow cooker chili is destined for rave reviews from your friends and family. Not only is it easy to make for just a few dollars per serving, it's also bold on flavor and great for big appetites. Shop for the best price on ground beef and chicken and choose the meat that saves you the most money. Serve with a topping of shredded cheddar cheese and a side of fluffy, baked rolls.

Yield: 6 servings

1 pound lean ground turkey

1 medium green pepper, finely chopped

1 small red onion, finely chopped

2 garlic cloves, minced

1 (28-ounce) can diced tomatoes, undrained

1 (16-ounce) can kidney beans, rinsed and drained

1 (14.5-ounce) can chicken broth

1 (6-ounce) can tomato paste

1 tablespoon chili powder

½ teaspoon pepper

1 teaspoon hot sauce

¼ teaspoon ground cumin

In a large skillet, cook the turkey, green pepper, and onion over medium heat until meat is no longer pink. Add garlic; cook 1 minute longer. Drain. Transfer to a slow cooker. Stir in the remaining ingredients. Cover and cook on low for 4 to 5 hours or until heated through.

Resist the temptation to throw away vegetables as soon as they begin to whither or brown. Chop off the good parts and use them in a stir-fry or stew, or bag them for later use.

Hearty Veggie & Bean Soup

This veggie and bean soup is the ultimate in low-maintenance Dollar Saving Dinners. Just dump everything in the slow cooker and let it simmer on low all day. The protein-packed beans will leave you feeling full and satisfied. Serve with crusty bread and relish every delicious spoonful, knowing that you've spent wisely.

Yield: 6 servings

5 cups vegetable or chicken broth

1 potato, cut into cubes

2 medium carrots, chopped (about 1 cup)

1 large onion, chopped (about 1 cup)

1 zucchini, chopped (about 1 cup)

3 tablespoons tomato paste

1 teaspoon salt

1 teaspoon Italian seasoning

½ teaspoon pepper

2 (15-ounce) cans pinto beans

1 (14-ounce) can diced tomatoes

BEST Bargain Alert $1.32 per serving!

Add all ingredients to slow cooker except diced tomatoes. Cover; cook on low 8 to 10 hours. Stir in diced tomatoes. Increase heat to high; cover and cook about 15 minutes longer.

Santa Fe Soup

A meat-lovers delight, this chunky Santa Fe Soup packs a whole lot of protein into every bowl. It's also a breeze to make in the slow cooker and stays delicious when reheated. Serve it with halves of grilled cheese sandwiches for the ultimate comfort food combo.

Yield: 6 servings

1 pound ground beef

3 (14.5-ounce) cans diced tomatoes, undrained

1 (15-ounce) can pinto beans, rinsed and drained

1 (15-ounce) can black beans, rinsed and drained

1 (15-ounce) can corn, undrained

1 cup salsa

1 (1-ounce) packet ranch dressing mix

1 (1.25-ounce) packet taco seasoning

1 cup shredded cheese

Dash fresh cilantro (for garnish)

In a skillet, brown meat and drain. Place in slow cooker or heavy-bottomed pot. Add in tomatoes, pinto beans, black beans, corn, salsa, ranch dressing mix, and taco seasoning and gently mix. Simmer on low heat for 20 to 30 minutes or until heated through. Serve with a topping of shredded cheese and a sprinkle of cilantro.

Add rice to your homemade soups to make them more filling without adding much to the cost.

Beef Bourguignon

It's not easy to stay on budget when you're cooking with beef, but it is possible. This recipe delivers on the promise of savory Beef Bourguignon without overdoing it on expensive ingredients. Look for chuck meat from your grocer, which is often less expensive, and buy in large portions so you can get the most for your money. It's also wise to purchase a whole chuck shoulder roast on sale and cut it into cubes yourself instead of paying for that convenience at retail. Freeze your leftovers to enjoy another day.

Yield: 6 servings

1½ pounds beef stew meat, cubed

¾ teaspoon salt

¾ teaspoon pepper

3 tablespoons all-purpose flour

3 cups beef broth, divided

¾ pound medium fresh mushrooms, quartered

1 cup pearl onions

2 medium carrots, sliced

1 (16-ounce) can red beans

2 garlic cloves, minced

2 tablespoons Italian tomato paste

1 bay leaf

1 teaspoon dried thyme

Sprinkle beef with salt and pepper. Coat a large nonstick skillet in cooking spray and brown beef in batches. Remove browned beef with a slotted spoon and place in slow cooker. Add flour; toss to coat. Add 2½ cups broth. In the same skillet, add the mushrooms, onion, carrots, and beans and cook 5 minutes. Add garlic; cook 1 minute longer. Add remaining broth, stirring to loosen browned bits from pan; stir in tomato paste. Transfer to slow cooker. Cover and cook on low for 8 to 10 hours or until beef is tender. Sprinkle with bay leaf and thyme and serve.

CHAPTER SIX

SANDWICHES, SALADS, AND MORE

Sloppy Joes

This sandwich is packed with so much flavor that we can forgive it for being just a little messy. The key to the ultimate Sloppy Joe is finding just the right barbecue sauce to suit your tastes: whether it's smoky, honey-flavored, or red hot, it's going to determine the fate of your Sloppy Joe, so choose wisely. Serve these tantalizing ground beef burgers with a side of coleslaw and some fries.

Yield: 4 servings

1 pound ground beef

1 small onion, chopped

1 (8-ounce) can tomato sauce

¼ cup ketchup

¼ cup barbecue sauce

1 tablespoon firmly packed brown sugar

1 teaspoon Dijon mustard

Salt and pepper

1 tablespoon Worcestershire sauce

1 tablespoon vinegar

4 hamburger rolls

In a large skillet, brown ground beef and onion. Drain. Stir in remaining ingredients. Cover and simmer for 15 to 20 minutes, stirring occasionally. Serve on toasted rolls.

Liven up affordable foods like pasta and potatoes with exciting blends of spices and you won't feel like you're eating on a budget.

Ground Turkey Tacos

Because it's both affordable and versatile as a dinner ingredient, ground turkey should be a dollar-saving staple in your refrigerator. These turkey tacos are as tasty as they are cost-effective. Serve them with your favorite assortment of toppings and enjoy.

Yield: 4 servings

1 pound ground turkey

½ teaspoon chili powder

¼ teaspoon cumin

½ teaspoon kosher salt

8 taco shells

1 small head romaine lettuce

1 beefsteak tomato, diced

1 red onion, sliced

1 (8-ounce) can corn "niblets"

1½ cups shredded cheddar (optional)

Cook ground turkey in a medium-size skillet over medium-high heat for 5 to 7 minutes, or until no longer pink. Stir in the chili powder, cumin, and salt. Line the bottom of each taco shell with a large leaf of lettuce. Spoon the turkey filling into the taco shells and top with tomato, red onion, and a sprinkle of corn. Add cheese if desired.

Pulled Pork Sandwiches

Whether you use your slow cooker or your oven, this recipe turns a dry pork shoulder (bought on sale of course) into heaps of tender, honey-flavored meat that melt in your mouth. Serve with a pickle and a side of coleslaw.

Yield: 4 servings

3 tablespoons paprika

1 tablespoon salt

2 teaspoons black pepper

½ teaspoon cayenne pepper

1 teaspoon garlic powder

½ teaspoon dried thyme

½ cup honey

¼ cup red wine vinegar

3 tablespoons olive oil

1 onion, peeled and cut in half

3–3½ pounds pork shoulder, cut in half

4 hamburger rolls

Whisk the first 6 ingredients in a mixing bowl. Add in the honey, vinegar, and olive oil and stir to make a paste. Place the onion in the bottom of an oven-safe dish or your slow cooker. Place the pork on top of the onion and cover with honey paste. Cook at 300°F in your oven or on low for 7 to 8 hours in your slow cooker until pork is easy to shred. Toast hamburger rolls and load with pulled pork.

Avoid overstuffing your fridge. Leaving enough room for air to circulate helps keep bacteria from growing and lengthens the life of your fresh food.

Blue Cheese Bacon Burgers

These incredible beef patties are loaded with blue cheese crumbles, caramelized onions, and crispy chunks of bacon. Whether you make them with frozen patties bought in bulk or ground beef purchased at sale price, topping them with this winning trio will feel like true indulgence.

Yield: 4 servings

2 tablespoons olive oil

2 large yellow onions, thinly sliced

½ tablespoon onion powder

½ teaspoon salt

½ teaspoon freshly ground black pepper

1 pound ground beef

1 (7-ounce) container blue cheese crumbles, or 1 cup chunky blue cheese dressing

6 slices thick-cut bacon, cooked and drained on paper towels

4 hamburger rolls, toasted

To caramelize the onions, heat olive oil in a large saucepan on medium heat. Add the onions, coat in olive oil and let cook about 20 minutes, stirring only as needed to prevent onions from sticking to pan and burning. Add more oil or water if needed. Once fully browned, remove onions from heat and set aside. In a large bowl, combine onion powder, salt, pepper, and use your hands to mix seasoning into ground beef. Form 4 similar-size patties. Preheat a skillet to high heat and cook patties on one side. Flip and cook for a minute, then add blue cheese crumble. Transfer cooked patties to toasted buns. Top each patty with ¼ caramelized onions and 1½ slices bacon (and blue cheese dressing if necessary).

Pre-formed burger patties, pre-sliced veggies, and chicken parts cost more than ground beef, whole veggies and whole chickens. Do your own portioning, chopping, and butchering, and you'll save on dinner before you even start cooking.

Bacon-Wrapped Dogs with Onions & Peppers

Who says you can't teach an old dog any new tricks? This dollar-saving dinner starts with a regular old hot dog, wraps it up in warm strips of bacon, and dresses it in onions and peppers. Serve with onion rings or french fries and watch them disappear.

Yield: 4–8 servings

8 slices thin-sliced bacon, uncooked

8 regular-size hot dogs

1 onion, diced

1 green bell pepper, diced

1 tablespoon olive oil

8 hot dog buns, toasted

Preheat oven to 400°F. Wrap bacon tightly around hot dogs; place on lined cookie sheet. Bake 10 to 15 minutes, or until bacon is fully cooked and hot dogs are browned. Meanwhile, cook diced onion and bell pepper in olive oil over medium heat until soft. Place cooked dogs in toasted buns and sprinkle with onions and peppers.

Meatball Submarine Sandwich

Made from scratch or from last night's leftover spaghetti dinner, meatballs are delicious served in a roll with cheese and extra sauce.

Yield: 4–6 servings

2 eggs, lightly beaten

¼ cup milk

½ cup dry breadcrumbs

2 tablespoons grated Parmesan cheese

½ teaspoon salt

¼ teaspoon pepper

⅛ teaspoon garlic powder

1½ pounds ground beef

2 tablespoons olive oil

6 sub rolls, toasted

1 (24-ounce) jar pasta sauce

½ pound provolone cheese, sliced

In a large bowl, whisk eggs and milk; mix in breadcrumbs, cheese, salt, pepper, and garlic powder. Add ground beef to breadcrumb mixture and mix in by hand. Shape into 2-inch meatballs. Preheat the oven to 350°F. Add olive oil to large saucepan and brown meatballs on all sides over medium-high heat. Place them on a greased cookie sheet and bake for about 15 minutes or until cooked through.

Serve 3 to 4 meatballs on each toasted roll, with ¾ cup pasta sauce (warmed in small saucepan) and 1 to 2 slices of provolone cheese.

Thanksgiving Sandwich

Sandwiches are a fantastic solution to the problem of lingering leftovers. Just layer on the very best that your fridge and pantry have to offer, and you haven't spent a dime on dinner! This sandwich is best when it's stacked high with all your favorite Thanksgiving offerings, including cranberry sauce, stuffing, and thick slices of turkey.

Yield: 4 servings

8 slices multigrain bread

1 pound roast turkey breast, thick sliced

4–6 tablespoons cranberry sauce

4–6 tablespoons mayonnaise

1 box stuffing mix, prepared

4 leaves lettuce

Toast bread if desired and warm turkey breast in the oven until heated through. Assemble sandwiches with ingredients listed and serve.

Chicken Parmesan Sandwich

Sweet tomato sauce meets warm, crunchy breaded chicken in this mouthwatering sandwich recipe. Using frozen chicken cutlets allows you to save heaps of money while cooking up an authentic, oven-fresh Chicken Parmesan Sandwich. For an even simpler version, use frozen chicken patties that are already breaded.

Yield: 4 servings

½ cup breadcrumbs

¼ cup grated Parmesan cheese

1 teaspoon Italian seasoning

¼ teaspoon salt

⅛ teaspoon fresh ground pepper

4 frozen, boneless, skinless chicken breast halves, thawed

1 egg, beaten

1 tablespoon cooking oil

1 cup tomato sauce

1 cup shredded mozzarella cheese

4 sub rolls

Preheat oven to 400°F. In a shallow bowl or pan, mix breadcrumbs, Parmesan cheese, oregano, basil, paprika, garlic powder, salt, and pepper. Dip each chicken breast in egg and dredge in the breadcrumb mixture. Heat oil in a skillet. Cook breaded chicken breast in batches over medium heat, about 4 minutes each side. Transfer cooked chicken to baking dish.

Cover each chicken breast with ¼ cup tomato sauce and ¼ cup cheese. Bake for 4 minutes. Add sub rolls to top shelf of oven and bake chicken 4 to 6 more minutes, or until cheese is melted and bread is toasted.

Crunchy Asian Chicken Salad

This recipe for Crunchy Asian Chicken Salad is love at first bite. The soy-marinated chicken strips are battered end-to-end in a crispy, fried coating. Serve them over a fresh bed of cabbage for a refreshing variation on your typical dinner salad. You can also use frozen breaded chicken strips and ready-made dressing for a quicker dinner.

Yield: 6 servings

DRESSING

1 garlic clove, finely minced

1 teaspoon ginger, finely minced

3 tablespoons rice vinegar

1 teaspoon soy sauce

1 teaspoon brown sugar

5 tablespoons canola oil

2 tablespoons sesame oil

1 tablespoon toasted sesame seeds

SALAD

6 egg whites

1½ cups soy sauce

6 chicken breasts or thighs (cut into 1- or 2-inch pieces)

2 cups flour

2 cups cornstarch

2 cups vegetable or canola oil

1 (16-ounce) bag coleslaw mix

Prepare the dressing: Place all ingredients in a food processor and blend until smooth. Keep in refrigerator until ready to use.

Cut chicken into 1- or 2-inch strips. Set aside.

Prepare the salad: Whisk together egg whites and soy sauce. Place chicken pieces in soy mixture and marinade for at least 20 minutes in refrigerator. Pour 1 cup flour and 1 cup cornstarch into a plastic freezer bag and shake until mixed. Add marinated chicken to bag in batches, shaking to coat. Replenish with remaining flour/cornstarch mixture as needed. Heat oil in wok or large skillet over high heat. Add chicken and fry 15 seconds. Set aside to cool on paper towels. Return to wok and fry an additional 15 to 20 seconds or until chicken is golden-hued and cooked through. Serve over coleslaw mix with sesame ginger dressing.

When putting away groceries, push new items to the back of your refrigerator shelves so that the old food gets eaten first.

Cobb Salad

A hearty dinner doesn't have to be strictly meat and potatoes. Try ending your day with the healthy crunch of this colorful Cobb Salad. Your taste buds will love the variety of textures and flavors, from salty feta crumble and buttery avocado to crunchy bacon. With this meal, it's crucial to buy your fruit and veggies fresh; but it's just as crucial to know what's in season, and to get the best price. Is the avocado too pricey in winter? Substitute some fresh celery and you're back on budget.

Yield: 3–4 servings

1 head romaine lettuce

1 avocado, chopped (optional)

2 fresh tomatoes, sliced

1 red onion, chopped

2 hardboiled eggs, sliced

¼ cup feta cheese, crumbled

3 slices cooked bacon

1 teaspoon olive oil

1 frozen chicken breast, thawed

Salt and pepper, to taste

Wash and drain lettuce, then break it up and place leaves in a large salad bowl. Add all toppings except for chicken to salad bowl. Gently toss. Cook chicken in oil in small saucepan. Sprinkle with salt and pepper. Slice into strips and serve warm over individual salad servings. Add your favorite dressing.

Chicken Alfredo Flatbread Pizza

Liven up pizza night with this unique gourmet chicken pizza with garlic Alfredo sauce. Instead of going to a restaurant and dropping an excessive amount of money on a similar indulgence, consider making this dollar-friendly Chicken Alfredo Flatbread Pizza at home.

Yield: 4 servings

1 pound frozen pizza dough, thawed

1 (15-ounce) jar Alfredo sauce

2 boneless, skinless chicken breasts, cooked and sliced

¼ cup roasted red peppers or fresh red pepper, chopped

1 cup shredded mozzarella cheese

2 tablespoons grated Parmesan cheese

1 tablespoon cracked black pepper

Heat oven to 425°F. Stretch pizza dough into a large, 12-inch circle on a lightly floured baking sheet or pizza stone; poke gently with fingertips to prevent air bubbles. Bake 10 minutes, then remove from oven. Spread Alfredo sauce onto pizza dough. Top with chicken and peppers. Sprinkle on shredded mozzarella, Parmesan, and black pepper. Bake 10 minutes more, or until cheese and crust begin to brown.

It can be tricky to compare prices when items are sold in varying amounts. Focus on the unit price sticker to determine the best value.

Index